FROM THE EARTH
How Resources Are Made

HOW NATURAL GAS IS FORMED

BY RYAN NAGELHOUT

Gareth Stevens
PUBLISHING

Please visit our website, www.garethstevens.com. For a free color catalog of all our high-quality books, call toll free 1-800-542-2595 or fax 1-877-542-2596.

Cataloging-in-Publication Data

Names: Nagelhout, Ryan.
Title: How natural gas is formed / Ryan Nagelhout.
Description: New York : Gareth Stevens Publishing, 2017. | Series: From the Earth: how resources are made | Includes index.
Identifiers: ISBN 9781482447163 (pbk.) | ISBN 9781482447187 (library bound) | ISBN 9781482447170 (6 pack)
Subjects: LCSH: Natural gas–Juvenile literature. | Gas as fuel–Juvenile literature. | Hydraulic fracturing–Juvenile literature.
Classification: LCC TP350.N34 2017 | DDC 553.2'85–dc23

Published in 2017 by
Gareth Stevens Publishing
111 East 14th Street, Suite 349
New York, NY 10003

Copyright © 2017 Gareth Stevens Publishing

Designer: Laura Bowen
Editor: Therese Shea

Photo credits: Cover, pp. 1–32 (title bar) Dimec/Shutterstock.com; cover, pp. 1–32 (text box) mattasbestos/Shutterstock.com; cover, pp. 1–32 (background) Alina G/Shutterstock.com; cover, p. 1 (gas burner) zkruger/Shutterstock.com; p. 5 Loadmaster/Wikimedia Commons; p. 7 (top) Daneil Novak/Moment/Getty Images; p. 7 (bottom) Tormod Sandtorv/Wikimedia Commons; p. 8 ggw1962/Shutterstock.com; p. 9 Charles Fenno Jacobs/The LIFE Images Collection/Getty Images; p. 11 (butane and ethane) molekuul_be/Shutterstock.com; p. 11 (propane and methane) ibreakstock/Shutterstock.com; p. 13 (coal formation) Spencer Sutton/Science Source/Getty Images; p. 13 (coal) SeDmi/Shutterstock.com; p. 13 (mine) Przemek Tokar/Shutterstock.com; p. 14 Juliar Studio/Shutterstock.com; p. 15 Meyers Konversationslexikon/Wikimedia Commons; p. 17 Bloomberg/Getty Images; p. 19 courtesy of NASA; p. 20 Joshua Doubek/Wikimedia Commons; p. 21 (top) jaddingt/Shutterstock.com; p. 21 (bottom) Denys Prykhodov/Shutterstock.com; p. 23 Harold Sund/Photographer's Choice/Getty Images; p. 25 SVF2/Universal Images Group/Getty Images; p. 27 Stockr/Shutterstock.com; p. 28 David McNew/AFP/Getty Images; p. 29 China Photos/Getty Images News/Getty Images.

Printed in the United States of America

CPSIA compliance information: Batch #CS16GS: For further information contact Gareth Stevens, New York, New York at 1-800-542-2595.

CONTENTS

Words in the glossary appear in **bold** type the first time they are used in the text.

WHAT IS GAS?

Gas is all around us. It's a state of matter, just like solids and liquids are. However, gas has no fixed shape and takes the form of whatever container it's in. Most gases can't be seen, but they're everywhere. They're in the air we breathe to live and even in the ground beneath us.

Much of that gas in the ground—loosely called natural gas—is very powerful. It can be used as a source of energy! How do we find natural gas in the ground? How do we get it out, and how do we use it?

WHAT'S IN AIR, ANYWAY?

People need the oxygen in air to survive, but it's not even the most plentiful gas in Earth's atmosphere. Nitrogen makes up about 78 percent of the atmosphere. Oxygen is second, making up nearly 21 percent of Earth's atmosphere. The gas argon makes up 0.93 percent, and tiny amounts of other gases such as carbon dioxide and neon are present as well.

other
argon
oxygen
nitrogen

Natural gas is an important source of fuel around the world, especially in the United States.

5

FINDING FLAMES

The first discoveries of natural gas seeps, or leaks, were made in the area that's now Iran between 6000 and 2000 BC. Around 1400 BC, the ancient Greek Temple of Apollo at Delphi was built on Mount Parnassus, the location of a natural gas flame. The oracle there was a priestess said to be able to tell the future. It's now believed she just thought she could because of the effect of the gas seep!

Around 200 BC, the Chinese drilled gas wells as deep as 500 feet (152 m). Bamboo pipes transported natural gas to the surface. It was used to boil water to make it drinkable.

ETERNAL FLAMES

Sometimes natural gas that reaches Earth's surface catches fire and creates what's called an eternal flame. Because they have a natural gas pocket fueling the flame, the fires can last for thousands of years! There are eternal flames all over the world, from a flickering flame behind a waterfall in western New York State to larger fires in Turkey and Australia!

Because natural gas can't be seen, flames fueled by natural gas and other fossil fuels in nature were once thought to be the work of gods or magic.

Eternal Flame Falls, Chestnut Ridge Park, NY

Door to Hell, Turkmenistan

In the United States, natural gas was first found by Native Americans. French explorers saw native peoples lighting gases near Lake Erie as early as 1626.

The first **commercialized** use of natural gas happened in Great Britain. Natural gas made from coal was used to light lamps on the street and also in homes around 1785.

In 1821, William Hart dug the first successful natural gas well in the United States in Fredonia, New York. His well became part of the Fredonia Gas Light Company, the first natural gas **distributor** in America. By 1836, the city of Philadelphia owned its own natural gas company.

HEAT AND COOKING

Natural gas was first used to light lamps, but the gas became more useful thanks to Robert Bunsen. In 1855, he invented a tool that combined natural gas and a certain amount of air to produce a hot flame. His Bunsen burner brought new uses for gas fuel: heating and cooking. The Bunsen burner is still used in labs and schools today.

The Philadelphia Gas Works is the biggest and oldest public gas system in the United States.

IT'S A MIXTURE

Natural gas isn't made of just one gas, but a collection of gases that have similar makeups. These gases are called hydrocarbons, which are compounds made with atoms of the elements carbon and hydrogen. Methane, for example, is a hydrocarbon with one carbon atom and four hydrogen atoms. It's the most abundant hydrocarbon found in natural gas.

Other hydrocarbons found in natural gas include ethane, propane, and butane. Each gas's **molecules** are made up of a different number of hydrogen and carbon atoms. Natural gas also contains some mixtures that aren't hydrocarbons, which are usually removed from the gas before it's used.

IN THE GROUND

Natural gas is most commonly found deep beneath Earth's surface, where rocks and pressure keep the gas beneath the air we breathe. If natural gas escapes the ground, however, it quickly rises. This is because natural gas is lighter than air. Natural gas also quickly dissipates, or spreads out, in air.

These are molecules of the different hydrocarbons that make up natural gas.

METHANE CH4

BUTANE C4H10

ETHANE C2H6

PROPANE C3H8

11

MAKING ENERGY

Like coal and oil, natural gas is a fossil fuel. "Fossil fuel" is the term used to describe burnable organic matter made of the remains of ancient plants and animals. When these organisms died, they were buried under layers and layers of sediment. The layers, sometimes hundreds or thousands of feet deep, applied great pressure and heat to the remains.

Over millions of years, these conditions transformed the plants and animals into fossil fuels. The kind of fossil fuel created depends on the type of buried matter, how long it was buried, and the amount of heat and pressure on it while it was decomposing, or breaking down.

CREATING COAL

The fossil fuel coal is made from the remains of trees, ferns, and other plants that died more than 250 million years ago. Like natural gas, heat and pressure also worked to create coal, which is usually found in places that were covered by water, such as swamps or bogs.

Coal Formation

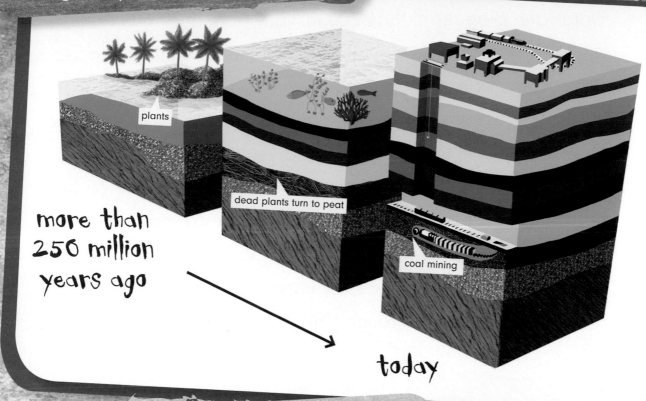

more than 250 million years ago

plants

dead plants turn to peat

coal mining

today

Animal and plant matter breaks down in the presence of oxygen, such as in the air we breathe. However, fossil fuels form when there's a lack of oxygen.

coal mine

coal

Oil and natural gas formed from organisms that lived in water and died more than 300 million years ago—even before dinosaurs existed. These watery areas included ancient oceans, seas, rivers, or sometimes even swamps. Organic matter was covered in ocean or river sediment, then heated and changed by bacteria over time.

In many places, this underground matter became oil and natural gas, which are often found together. Oil and natural gas traveled up to the surface through cracks over time. Sometimes they settled under cap rocks, or **impermeable** rocks that don't allow matter to seep through. This is called a sedimentary basin.

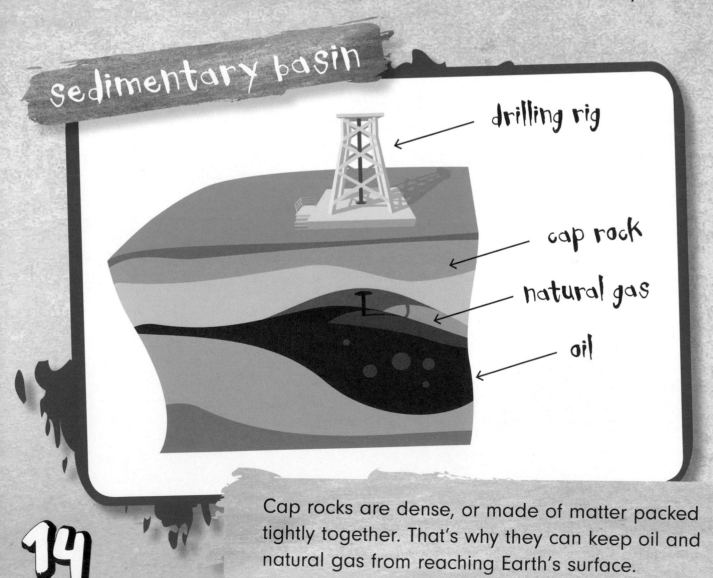

sedimentary basin

drilling rig

cap rock

natural gas

oil

Cap rocks are dense, or made of matter packed tightly together. That's why they can keep oil and natural gas from reaching Earth's surface.

ANAEROBIC DIGESTION

Fossil fuels are made in a process called anaerobic digestion. This is when organic matter decomposes in an **environment** without oxygen, resulting in carbon-rich matter that can be burned as fuel. If oxygen were present, the carbon would be turned into carbon dioxide.

15

WHERE IT'S FOUND

Natural gas **deposits** found closest to Earth's surface often contain more oil than natural gas. Larger pockets of natural gas are found deeper inside Earth, where higher temperatures and more pressure were put on organic matter over a longer period of time. Wells are drilled to collect natural gas and oil.

Natural gas is also found inside tiny pockets in soft rocks called shale. Freeing the gas from shale in large amounts requires different tools and processes. A special method called hydraulic fracturing, or hydrofracking, is one method of extracting, or removing, that gas.

ASSOCIATED PETROLEUM GAS

Associated petroleum gas (APG) is gas dissolved in, or mixed into, oil. It's made of light hydrocarbons, which are also found in natural gas, including methane, ethane, propane, and butane. APG is taken out of oil when it's **refined**. Companies sometimes burn off APG, resulting in pollution, but it can also be used to make some kinds of fuels.

FAST GAS FACTS: NATURAL GAS IS...

colorless

not toxic to humans in low amounts

lighter than air

naturally odorless

only ignites, or lights on fire, when the air and gas mixture contains between 5 and 15 percent natural gas

Where natural gas is found determines how it is reached and extracted by energy companies.

DRILLING FOR GAS

Natural gas makes up about 41 percent of the US energy supply. Almost all the natural gas used by the United States is found domestically, or within the country.

Before a company drills for gas, scientists use special tools to study where natural gas pockets are located underground. If they think there's enough natural gas for the company to make money, a production well is drilled straight down into the gas pocket. Raw natural gas flows up the well to the surface. Often large pumps are needed to force natural gas to the surface. Then the natural gas is processed.

FLARING

Sometimes natural gas found with other fossil fuels is flared, or burned off, at wells. Many scientists say this hurts the environment by releasing lots of carbon dioxide, a gas that contributes to global climate change. Well operators admit at least 0.13 percent of natural gas produced nationwide is vented or flared, but others say that percentage is even higher.

The lights in this image of North Dakota show mostly natural gas well sites and gas flaring.

Minot

Williston

NORTH DAKOTA

Dickinson

19

FRACKING

The hydrofracking process uses a mixture of materials to free natural gas from large shale formations deep underground. Wells are drilled down into the shale. Then drills are usually turned horizontally, too. A fracking liquid mixture—water, sand, and other chemicals—is sent down the well at high pressure.

The force of this liquid fractures the shale formation, freeing the bubbles of natural gas. It collects and then rises up the well. Most of the liquid is then taken out, though some is left behind. While some US states such as Oklahoma and Pennsylvania allow hydrofracking, other states such as New York have banned it.

drilling site

WASTEWATER DANGER

The liquid used in fracking needs to be treated after use, but sometimes it's just disposed of in underground wells thousands of feet deep. Scientists have noticed an increase in **earthquake** activity near these sites. People also worry about the effect of wastewater on drinking-water sources.

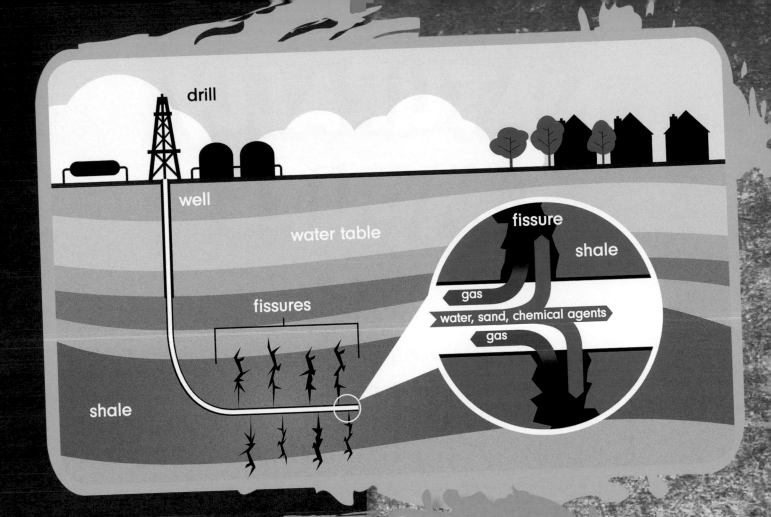

drill

well

water table

fissures

shale

fissure

shale

gas

water, sand, chemical agents

gas

Steps of Fracking

natural gas pipeline

1. Drill well down

2. Turn well horizontally

3. Water, sand, and chemicals pushed in

4. Shale breaks

5. Gas flows up well

People opposed to hydrofracking say it causes too many problems for the environment.

NATURALLY IMPURE

Raw natural gas has **impurities** that must be removed before it's used for heating and cooking. It's moved from wells through pipes to a processing plant. There, it's purified before it's moved over longer distances. Water and some gases are taken out through different processes.

Sometimes processing plants use gravity to pull heavier liquids and gases away from the natural gas. Once it's processed, the gas is sent through a network of pipes to storage places for later use. The smell some link to natural gas is added by gas companies so people know when they have a gas leak.

LIQUEFIED NATURAL GAS

Natural gas becomes a liquid when it's cooled to -260°F (-162°C). Liquefied natural gas (LNG) is clear and has 1/600 the volume of the fuel than its gas state, which makes it easier to ship a large amount of natural gas. Liquid natural gas also can't ignite, which makes moving it safe.

Natural gas may travel through thousands of miles of pipeline before being processed into a usable form at a plant like this one.

USING THE WASTE

What's left after processing natural gas depends on the kind of well it was taken from and what fuel source the energy company was looking for when drilling. But not all the gases and matter taken out of natural gas during processing are vented off or considered useless. In fact, some hydrocarbons and other gases are purified and used as fuels themselves.

Butane, propane, ethane, isobutane, and natural gasoline are all refined and sold by energy companies. Propane is used to power tools and heat grills, for example, and butane is often used in lighters.

HYDROGEN AND HELIUM

The two most common elements in the universe—hydrogen and helium—are often hard to find in gas form on Earth. Both hydrogen and helium are taken from natural gas. Helium is used for many things, from filling balloons to scientific experiments. Hydrogen is used for rocket fuel!

Some gases removed from natural gas are used to help companies retrieve oil in wells, refine oil, and produce chemicals.

METHANOGENS AND BIOFUEL

There's another, faster way to make natural gas: methanogens. These are microorganisms that live in the intestines of animals, including humans, as well as in places where there's little oxygen on Earth's surface, such as landfills where buried trash decomposes. Methanogens break matter down into a type of methane called biogenic methane. This process is called methanogenesis. Most of this methane escapes into the atmosphere, but scientists are working on ways to trap this gas for fuel use.

Other scientists are even working to turn human and animal waste into fuels called biofuels! This would help tackle many pollution problems.

GROWING GAS

Scientists and energy companies are testing a new energy source: biogas made with fast-growing algae. Algae are grown in giant tanks of water and then heated to make a synthetic, or man-made, biogas. This biofuel can be used to make fuel products such as the heavy oil diesel, gasoline for cars, and even jet fuel.

By finding new ways to produce natural gas and biofuels, scientists hope to reduce the need to take natural gas out of the ground in ways that may harm the environment.

27

YOU DECIDE

Natural gas is a major source of energy in the United States, but should that continue in the future? Some say burning fossil fuels harms the environment too much, that fossil fuels are a resource that will run out, and that hydrofracking methods are too dangerous.

Supporters of fossil fuels say there's plenty of natural gas left underground to supply energy for the United States for at least the next 60 years. They also say burning natural gas is better for the environment than the fossil fuels coal or oil. What do you think? Should we keep using natural gas for energy?

BLOWOUTS

In 2015, a well blowout, or an uncontrolled release, at a natural gas storage facility near Los Angeles, California, forced thousands of people from their homes. The leak lasted 16 weeks and sent 107,000 tons (97,069 mt) of methane into the air. Many point to accidents like these when complaining about the use of fossil fuels.

Porter Ranch community, near well blowout

Burning natural gas releases almost 30 percent less carbon dioxide than burning oil and 45 percent less carbon dioxide than burning coal. Too much carbon dioxide in the atmosphere is linked to global climate change.

29

GLOSSARY

associated: found alongside something else

bog: a poorly drained area rich in plant life and often surrounded by water

climate change: long-term change in Earth's climate, caused partly by human activities such as burning oil and natural gas

commercialized: caused to be sold to produce income

deposit: an amount of matter in the ground that built up over a period of time

distributor: a person or company that supplies stores or businesses with goods

earthquake: a shaking or trembling of part of Earth's surface

environment: everything that surrounds a living thing

impermeable: unable to be passed through

impurity: something unwanted that is mixed in with something else

molecule: a group of atoms of one or more elements bound to each other

refine: to make better or more pure

FOR MORE INFORMATION

BOOKS

Bailey, Diane. *Natural Gas Power*. Mankato, MN: Creative Education, 2015.

Chambers, Catherine. *How Harmful Are Fossil Fuels?* Chicago, IL: Capstone Heinemann Library, 2015.

Parker, Steve. *Natural Gas*. Broomall, PA: Mason Crest, 2015.

WEBSITES

Fossil Fuel Energy
kidzworld.com/article/1423-fossil-fuel-energy
Learn more about natural gas and other fossil fuels here.

Kids and Natural Gas Safety
www.aga.org/video-kids-and-natural-gas-safety
Watch videos and learn how to stay safe around natural gas on this site.

Natural Gas Basics
eia.gov/kids/energy.cfm?page=natural_gas_home-basics
Learn more about natural gas and how it's made here.

INDEX